Captain Kintail

Also by John Terpstra:

Scrabbling for Repose
Forty Days and Forty Nights
Naked Trees

Captain Kintail

John Terpstra

Netherlandic Press, 1992
Windsor, Ontario, Canada

PUBLISHED BY Netherlandic Press, P.O. Box 396, Station A, Windsor, Ontario, Canada N9A 6L7.
THE PUBLISHER WISHES to acknowledge the generous support of the Canada Council and the Ontario Arts Council — Joan Magee, Publisher.
THANKS TO Gerard Brender à Brandis for his permission to reproduce the wood engraving 'Tulip' for the back cover of this book.
TYPESET IN Monotype Sabon by Peter Enneson Design Inc. (Toronto). Cover and Typographic Design, Peter Enneson PRINTED ON Zephyr Antique laid, sewn into signatures and bound by The Porcupine's Quill, Inc.

Canadian Cataloguing in Publication Data
Terpstra, John
    Captain Kintail

Poems
ISBN 0-919417-27-2

I. Title.

PS8589.E75C3 1992   C811'.54   C92-094953-3
PR9199.3.T47C3 1992

This book is for everyone at St. Cuthbert's.

(A weekend get-together, in late June, at a lakeside camp.
A summer camp, in the traditional sense: large dining hall, with
attached bunkrooms & counsellor quarters; a few cabins close by, in
the trees — each with a long Indian name carved or painted above
the doorway.

Though still standing, with its view of the lake, the old wooden
dining hall has been replaced by one made of concrete & steel,
which has the look & feel of an airplane hangar.

Enter the group that has reserved the camp for this weekend — their
seasonal retreat.

It rains.)

Captain Kintail lets the screen door slam,
"There's not one cabbage to be found in all of Kincardine."
That's Frank, of course, back with the groceries,
but missing a few heads.

                               "Somebody, *write that down*,"
says Suzanne, to which Ron, drawing deeply from his bank
of epigrams, replies, "Words falsify reality."
So where's *his* head?

Oh, look out! Fasten
your seatbelts, we're taking off. And let's step on it,
let's tear up the narrow road that threads
the lovely and serene mennonite countryside, and go
where Frank has called us. Frank the organizer,
the shepherd, who gathers all of the ninety-and-nine
who'll sign up, each year, at this time,
for the windward side of holy Lake Huron, to camp
just down the road from a town called Kintail,
a town too small for shopping, which is why he's back
from Kincardine, lacking the cabbages, though it's more
kith than kin in this cabbageless patch we hightail it to,
free of the city and our private lives, for a few
last days, this last long weekend of Spring,
when the endless pilgrimage of winter is really over,
and the pursed lips of every branch have already opened
into the kisses of Summer. Yes, the leaves are out.
We greet the saints: the trees, the lake.
And slow down already. We made it.
We're here.
                There's lots of time.

But slow is right, for it will rain, rain,
day and night, drip and drizzle, downpour,
for in the press of last minute details
someone forgot to pack the weather.

                                        He leadeth us,
he feedeth us,
                to him
we shall complain.
                        Frank!?

CAUTION: Horsedrawn vehicles use this road,
says Menno, holding up the signpost.

And the rain will be amplified on the roof
over the dining hall all that first evening,
its volume cranked up so it takes a while
to convince the kids and tuck them in
to someplace new. And someone will light a fire,
and as the tot socks and sneakers hang to smoke dry
someone else will say that this recalls
the Iroquois longhouses they saw rebuilt
at Crawford Lake, with poles and bark, and roots
for lashing, and that the homes were not this wide,
but higher, and domiciled several families, and all ages,
from pipsqueak to grandam, for twenty years,
before they folded, into
the earth.

       "That must have been fun," pipes little Ann,
"can *we* stay here *all* the time?"

And later on
tables will be shoved across the floor, chairs set,
and the board games will unfold, the picture games,
word games, in which we envision and invent
our own definitions, these last few days, this last
long weekend of Spring, before the break
to Summer, and we'll play to the present
sounds of nature, that echo
off the roof, that fill this cavern
of concrete block, and ricochet the walls
up and down the narrower cavern hallways, leading
to the bunkrooms —
                              someone's left the door open.
They flood back in.
                              "Daddy, I have to pee."
The kids are so juiced for this weekend.
                                                    Come,
lie down, little lamb.
                              "But I'm afraid."
Be not. Remember, Noah floated. And if it
comes to that, so will we. We're safe.
Lie down. You're safe
inside.

BALDERDASH! says Milton Bradley,
eavesdropping spokesman for the sopping world
at large: Just who decides which are the goats
that'll never make it with your sheep? Mercy!
please. We're in this, all together, lamb and kid,
float
        or sink — it's in the genes. Open up.
New word: think, "geep".

New words

confirm

or falsify.

So where's *his* head?

And the last car
of those who elected to come
pulls into the parking lot past midnight.
The cavern is quiet, the children all sleep,
but our gepherd knows his geep, that this lot's
revved-up by the drive, wants to frolic.
While others slumber he leads these three or four
through an open window in the clouds, down
to the water, and by the moon, where they will build
a second fire, of driftwood, flotsam
in the life of a lake, what
the lake retrieves

                    holy

                            and for a while
they will forget what's what, the clock,
that ticking observation of ourselves,
the blanket urgencies that cover us, would save,
that plot our habitation on the planet, our days,
and they will abandon all

                            to dance
themselves and us

                        upon that point
between the walls of wave and cedar.

And the water says

refresh

refresh

And it will sound like the kids again,
their voices bouncing off the cavern walls
when they flood back in, four a.m.

                              Somebody,
write this down:
                    this shared accomodation
of distinct individuals, singles,
several families, all ages,
                         and the similar nights
we're wide awake, and hearing voices, listening
for our name, while the earth's other half
keeps watch,
                these foreign snores
from someone-in-the-next-room's deep,
                                        snorkles
from the long lake they're crossing; the dreams
and nightmares of other's children,
their little factories of toes and fingers
making noise,
              pipsqueaks,
like the very early morning sounds
from under the soffits
      in the trees,
                    how very vulnerable
each night
            we volunteer to sleep.

And in the morning the children will run
through a drizzle they don't mind
to tell about the big fish on the beach
and the seagulls picking at it. That's
nature. *Gross.* And they will run
right to the edge of the water
where the waves are slurping at their feet,
attracted to it, while the seagulls wait
in the wind for something to happen.

But nothing like that will happen this weekend,
none will go missing, not one hauls off
down the drink, though they're off, unseen,
all day, through the bush, the field, the beach,
though Marty will say, "Maybe it's the seven years
we lived in Detroit, when it was called Murder City,
but I hate to let them out of my sight."

And there will be more talk this weekend, tales
of the near hit, of accidents, or the recent persistent
conniving pain, the lump under there, the sudden
slow death of parents,
                              and talk
of how impossible or not it is to dodge
these standard random shots
that are fired from who knows where
but seem so well attracted to human flesh, can come
through any window, plate glass, stained, or the old
wavey kind from grandam's house, and shatter
the held familiar view, and lodge in the body, or maybe
only the wall this once, but delivering a fright,
and driving those glittering slivers of hot
compressed sand into the skin,
where they just burrow deeper,

                                        as if to find
an ever safe inside.

Someone toddles in for a nap.

Is it that late already?
Lie down, little lamb.

And the rain will confirm
a kind of reality within this cavernous hall,
its echo amplify

          our current preferred building methods,
choice of materials, our code requirements
for concrete block, steel truss, and the zero-
slope roofline,

        like a bunker's, hunched
low to the ground, sieged against
the earth, the sky, expecting

             sirens:
it takes the tiniest fears and bops
them off the walls like pingpong balls
in a box.

       You must talk softly.
Don't think aloud.

Say what?

The lights go out.

Is everyone okay?

Is anyone

not hurt,
afraid?

But the light returns, and the windows hold,
and it's still only the last long weekend of Spring,
and time is flying, as usual, it flitters and pops
like a moth against the bulb, and our lives are only,
after all, slowly dimming, like the days
to come:
Summer's next week.

Mercy!
So where's *his* head?

And so we will finally break, I suppose,
I *hope*, and take off to escape the weather
within, seek cloud cover, direct precipitation,
feeling it on the face, unechoed,
and pouring throught the roof,

      cumulus. That's
nature,
   human's, trying to lighten up;
and headed down the path in rivulets,

       water's
slurped beneath the bottom step. "That's
the old bunkhouse," says Wayne, "The last year
I camp-counselled here, they abandoned it
for the new one up the hill."

       And so it swallows
continuous mouthfuls now
of streaming rain, grows sodden
round the foundation, is given to rot
and remembering
     the many summer coats of paint,
the soft shell of lap siding, and all
carved initials, deep affections
worked into the grain —

      is taking them with, it goes
with this decline,
    and won't be shored against
a listing toward the cedar slope, folding itself
for a slide into the lake.

     It desires
to be driftwood, someday.
      holy

Something like that will happen.

Our bunker's up,
of course, on higher ground, is intended to always
go no place. That's instituted, six feet down.
This perfect ugliness is built to last
till we're all below grade.

Frank!?

Ding   Ding.

Is it that time already?

                      And the geep will be called
from the fields, the beach, to gather out of the rain,
shove chairs and tables, and find their place within
the loudness, the hungry confusion, for lunch, under
the only shelter we've got — so lighten up, already —
and it's only once we're sitting
and the cups and plates are being passed
that we notice what's cooking, who's
to the right, who's left, who's dawdled
out of doors.

               All seats reserved
for anyone, says someone.

                      And our gepherd stands,
off in the corner, arms folded, wearing his wild grin.
He's in his element. He's just so glad
this crowd's come out, that the weekend's not
a flop, he doesn't care
where we are, who's
we, or where their butts are finally parked;

                            these little ones,

for whom, for now, it seems
the earth's at last enough,

                their most common ground.

And nature's act will clean it up this weekend,
and the children will rush in to tell
about the big fish on the beach
that's gotten smaller, is only
head and tail,
                    its inner life
transfigured, ascended into heaven
with the birds of the air.

And washing the dishes,
Ann will flip consecutive clean plates my way, and say,
"It doesn't happen often, but when George
gets mad, he gets bigger. It's scary.
I feel sorry for those guys
he's up against, in Thunder Bay."
And given his physique, it's probably
to mythological proportions that he grows.
No offense. It suits the lake. His job is,
he maps Ojibway paths to higher ground, where
they don't build, but greet the clouds, the maker,
individually

       envision time and place, call
the long names, become a people
seeing roots

     draw

        on the long lie-down
of elders under the earth, the sky,
unsieged;

and would we could be them, be *him*,
by George, and outgrow all enclosure, the confines
of the Hearing Room, bulge windows
from their frame and talk a body
language those lifeless landgrabbing
bigwigs can maybe understand, larger
than one of their deals, their mines,
their dams
              and dance on a point
between the walls of wave and cedar.

May I?

music, please.

                                    And later that evening
Peter will hear two guitars tuning together
by the fire. And he will whisper, "I hope
they don't play 'Heart of Gold'." For it seems
wherever two or three guitars are gathered, there is
'Heart of Gold'. His whisper, however, no sooner
said, but pongs across the room, translating
to request:
                    'I want to live, I want to give,
                    I've been a miner for a heart of gold.'
Listen, Peter: recognize that drone? Not
Neil's singing, but where he took it from:
perpetual rain, or the low volume
of everyday, when even what
you do with pride or passion
wearies, and you hear that white noise
loneliness,
                    the background sound
that slowly overcomes all tune, grows
deafening, it won't let up, moves
nearer to home...
                    is where
the heart? you'll sometimes wonder,
                                        until you wake
one morning, crawl all fours to the cellar, map
a path to that northwest corner, where's
safe,
        where's dry, and curl
in a very traditional pose.

Mother of God,
it can come to that,
this native being
alone inside.

live   give

And the story will come down to us this Summer
that a small town flooded, and a ten-year-old was taken
by the wild white of water at the side of the road.
They saw her rushed through the open grate, into
the culvert, and screamed for her, small and lost
within cascading concrete. Someone wanted
to go in after, but it was hopeless.
They had to wait. It took
all afternoon and evening
for the raging to abate.

                        Her parents
couldn't rest, of course, but only think
our little girl, and remember
with a single-noted vividness
everything she'd ever said or done, what
she'd given them, what they'd returned
in love or fear or anger.

                       Come morning,
and she'd grown larger
than she ever was, or, perhaps
than they could ever let her,

                       and they found her,
then, that morning, alive, but cold,
and scratched, bruised, with stiff limbs
from how she'd clung to the barest crack
in the concrete, waiting, a crack
their adult fingers
couldn't grasp.

                "I heard my name," she whispered,
"inside the water. Mummy,

                     I never was afraid."

And on the last morning of that last long weekend
of Spring, before take-off, before we break
camp for Summer, someone will sit a baby
on the beach. The rain's let up, at long last,
so gather round, and we will dig a puddle
at his feet, pour portions of the lake therein,
and watch the pipsqueak dunk and play as the walls
go up and the moat fills and the twigs
begin to flutter from the turrets.
And this compulsion will not go unrecognized,
and a certain giddy behaviour will overcome
the inhabitants at this point on the planet
as we work and sing and the kid is enclosed
most beautifully.

Hold it, folks.

A camera clicks.

Somewhere in there is baby Chris.

And the water says

                          retrieve

                                    refresh

and rounds the castle sand, its hand
the gentle one that also roams his hips.

And another story will come down to us this summer,
that twenty years ago, give or take,
it was just the two of them, living
on the moon, domiciled in a small room,
one window, on stilts:
a precarious existence.
                    They lasted out
their weekend, then left
that garden of dust, but when
they first arrived, remember
how everyone went out, looked up?
The earth was all eyes that evening,
                              and the sky,
and the two were far and away
too small and lost
for us to see, but they asked
if you recall, for a moment of silence,
and now Buzz says that as the quiet grew
enveloping he'd never felt
so strong the sense he was
                    a part,
which is when he ate the piece of bread,
and the wine, he said, sort of floated in the cup.

It's almost time. We leave at noon.

                                   And right on cue
someone will open a plastic bag, and the kids will rush
to grab, and stuff some in their mouths, and break
the rest, tossing pieces in the air, over the water,
gathering seagulls as we pack to go,
as we dwell, already,
on the afterlife
of briefly living here,

                         envisioning
the long trips,

                  inventing home,
this planet that we come from.

"Look out, people,"
says Ruth, "Someone's been writing this down."

And where we ever were
our footprints are,

        like on the moon.

But this coming Summer could, of course,
totally eclipse our weekend and the moon.
Summer's like that, once the sun wins out.
And we can always question how and why,
whatever the weather, what precipitates, and if
the moon's a place
                        whose influence is over
the lake, the waves
                        of doubt and pleasure
we dance,
            and begin the pilgrimage again.

Captain Kintail's taking names.
We know where's *his* head:
same time, same place, next Spring.

And counting down the kilometres from camp
a family pulls into the station. I'm at
the pump, tanking gas into a car
thirsty for the lake, and thinking how best
to rethread the mennonite countryside home,
when a fellow ambles up.
                                "How about
that rain?" he asks. His grandam stitched
and placed it on his chest: Barry

this isn't self-serve?

     "No, sir," he says,

   "it ain't."

Words confirm reality.

Someone, I trust, is keeping a record of this.

NOTES:

Edward "Buzz" Aldrin only recently made public the contents of the personal pack (which each astronaut is allowed) that he carried on board the Apollo 11 flight, and when the Eagle landed.

Milton Bradley *makes and sells* BALDERDASH, *a word definition game. One of the words players may have to invent a meaning for is "geep" — the actual name for a goat/sheep hybrid.*

George McKibbon, *a land-use planner, spends much time in Northern Ontario, where he maps areas that are significant, or sacred, to the various Ojibway & Cree bands who live there. He uses these maps while advocating on behalf of the bands, at hearings with the Ministry of Natural Resources & the commercial interests that wish to log, mine or develop hydro-electricity.*

Menno *Simons (1496-1561) begat the Mennonites, Protestant Christians who still "lead lives of great simplicity, both secularly & religiously," and often live in separate communities.*

Frank, Suzanne, Ron, *little* Ann, Marty, Wayne, Ann, Peter, *baby* Chris *&* Ruth *are, always, only themselves.*

Captain Kintail won the 1992 CBC Radio Literary Competition.
It was recorded and aired on the CBC/FM program *Writers & Co.*

JOHN TERPSTRA is a Canadian-born writer whose family came to
Canada from Friesland, The Netherlands, shortly after the Second
World War, settling in Brockville, Ontario. He has also lived in
Edmonton, Chicago, Toronto, and Midland Park, New Jersey, and
presently lives in Hamilton with his wife and two daughters, where
he works as a cabinetmaker.

HIS PREVIOUS COLLECTIONS of poetry include *Scrabbling for
Repose* (Split Reed Press, 1982), *Forty Days and Forty Nights*
(Netherlandic Press, 1987), and *Naked Trees* (Netherlandic Press,
1990). *Forty Days and Forty Nights* received the Bressani Award
for poetry in 1988.